God Cries and An Angel Loses Its Wings

How building relationships with your
customers, can grow your business and
create community

Frank Lanzkron-Tamarazo

Dedication

To my wife, Lisa, who has suffered throughout the years with the repeated pain of hearing me tell the stories in this book.

To my beautiful children, Max, Doris, and Nicoletta.

To my mother, Doris, of blessed memory, who loved me more than any only child could possibly deserve.

To my father, Nick, of blessed memory, who taught me to

Keep your ears open

your eyes open

and your mouth shut.

Table of Contents

Acknowledgments

Many thanks to the continually nagging presence of Robert Palmer of Raven Writing Studios, INK. Without his guidance, I would not have had the courage to finish this book.

Thank you to Myndi Weinraub who graciously took the mantle of copy editor for my book. She was referred by a social media maven and fellow author, Don Kowalewski, who inspired me to self publish my first book.

The cover illustration was created by Vincent Tozzo, a crazy talented illustrator and artist. Many thanks to Edward and Angela Marsh of NightCry Graphics who are my graphic designer muses. Thank you to Brian of Progress Custom Design in Ferndale, Michigan, for your assistance with the awesome cover.

There is great truth behind the fact that behind every successful man is a great wife. That great wife is Lisa Lanzkron-Tamarazo who has been my best friend for over 25 years. We have shared a quarter century in laughter, tears, and occasional mockery.

Many thanks to my favorite kids, Max, Doris, and Nicoletta, who keep me humble, entertained, and happy.

Introduction

My wife, Lisa, and I spent our life savings to start and sustain a business, Chazzano Coffee Roasters. Before that leap of faith, I was full-time clergy, a Cantor at various synagogues for 15 years. I also had more than 10 years of coffee roasting experience but no real business experience. With a new business passion acquired, I read every book on the subject I could get my hands on and studied my way to success. I went into this endeavor with what I consider some great assets- a supportive wife, a crazy sense of humor, tremendous self-confidence, a passion for the industry and a love for teaching it to others, strong interpersonal skills and a rosy, optimistic view of life. I've also inherited a congenital loss of hearing, so I come off as an incredible listener, even when I'm just very focused. There are other qualities that have been helpful, and they are all teachable. That's the wisdom I want to impart to you with this book. Through my successes and stumbles, wins and losses, I think I have a lot to share that can help you grow as a person, businessperson, even a leader of your synagogue or church with easy to learn tools.

Throughout the day, I make it a habit to teach customers, business friends, my children, or my employees about something I find important. I want to share this unique world view that I have acquired. My evolution as a business man began with my life as a Cantor- that series of experiences helped me grow Chazzano Coffee Roasters. Conversely, my successful business life taught me strategies to improve the synagogues that I used to serve full-time.

When a customer orders coffee in my cafe, and asks for sugar or cream in their coffee, there is sometimes a collective intake of breath from other customers. The other customers sometimes smirk knowingly- they know what words are going to come out of my smiling mouth. It's similar to that old E.F. Hutton commercial where all of the customers in a busy restaurant stop talking and there's complete silence. So when a customer asks for sugar for their coffee, we say, "You should try it first. If it's really great coffee, you don't need sugar. Wine has 750 different flavor profiles while coffee has over 1500. This coffee has the following notes..." If they seem to have a good sense of humor, then the punch line that everyone is waiting for is unleashed: "And you know, if you put sugar or cream in my coffee, G-d cries and an angel loses its wings."

This is a very common occurrence at the cafe- this exchange could happen several times each hour on a busy day. What did we just do for the customer and for the business? Allow me to dissect the carefully orchestrated scene. The new customer asks for cream and sugar. Most coffee shops would say, "Sure, here you go" without any explanation. However, we want the customer to understand the ramifications of adding anything to the coffee. We're demonstrating that this is a special product, and sugar will only mask its natural flavor. It's not a regular cup of coffee. (In fact, there's no such thing as far as I'm concerned!) When someone asks for a regular cup of coffee, we joke that we don't have regular cups of coffee. This is the best cup of coffee you'll ever taste. Again, we're adding value, even an educational component to the experience. It's obvious we really believe in what we're doing.

Once they're in on the joke, the regular customer now feels like they are part of the business. They have a sense of ownership and they become evangelists and fellow teachers. Where else can you go where a regular customer tells a new customer: "You want to try it before you put sugar in it. I used to put sugar in my coffee two years ago, but now I drink it black." It sounds more like an AA meeting than a coffee shop. What happens when the customer tastes the coffee, and behold, they find out they really don't need the sugar, and they really can enjoy their coffee black? You now have a customer for life. You've taught them something new. You may have also ruined their lives in a funny way. Where else can they receive that same amount of care, education, and personal assistance? They'll remember Chazzano Coffee as the first place they drank their coffee black. Maybe even tell their friends about the owner's funny "angel" line. Then they'll bring their friends in and ask you to tell them the joke, and give them the spiel.

This book will teach you how to both educate and interview your customers, create community in your business, and create a better life for you and your family.

Chazzano Coffee Roasters has a large regular customer base because we make them part of the family. How often are you invited by the owner or employee to tour the facility? You came in to buy a cup of coffee and the owner takes a few minutes while your coffee is brewing to share his passion for coffee with you? How crazy is that? Crazy like a fox, my father would often say. Next time you are craving a cup of coffee, where are you going to go? You'll probably go out of your way to go to the place where you felt at home. You visited the "holy" bean room, as I am wont to say. After I talk about Chazzano Coffee and the cafe, I always ask, "So, what do you do? What's your target market? What do you want to do?"

While you sip your coffee or tea at the cafe, we'll come by and ask, "How's the coffee/tea?" Then we'll give you samples of other coffees or teas, brewed in different ways. Remember the story about Abraham and the three angels? It is one of my favorite Bible stories because it teaches us about the role of guest and host. Abraham sees three men (really, angels) coming towards him. He immediately rises to greet them and offers them food and beverages (not Chazzano Coffee). Treat your business as if your customers are really guests at your house. Engage them in conversation if they are open to that. Find out what they do for a living, what their target market is, and what you can do to help grow their business and their life. Make them smile by smiling and telling short jokes. Make them feel like this is their second home.

Building a business is fundamentally about reducing costs and growing profitability so that there is more revenue in your pocket. However, there are ways to accomplish that while you grow your life and there are ways to accomplish that while simultaneously hurting your social and emotional well-being.

When I first opened the cafe, I met a baker who had a great product and loyal customer following, but he was always miserable. There was always a frown on his face and when he did attempt a smile, it failed. The reason was that he had been baking all day long for the past 5 years. It took up his entire life. He was depressed because he didn't see the light out of this job that he'd made for himself. He had little time for family; no balance. Sadly, I have found too many people who live this life. They realize their passion, build a business, but they don't have an exit strategy for themselves. They don't delegate themselves out of a job and make themselves the visionary for their business venture. They just sink deeper into the hole. They may even be making money, but they hate their lives and therefore their passion for the business is dying. That scenario just makes me weep. I look at those people and I say, That will never happen to me. I am confident in that belief because the title of the book, Small Business, Big Life is the business religion that I meditate upon every day. The main idea of the book is that you build up your small business, ONLY to attain the Big Life. It's great when a small business becomes a big business, but only when it enriches your life in the process.

If you're missing your kids' ball games, recitals, or developmental milestones, or haven't had a date with your wife for months, or you rarely smile, you're a failure. There's hope for you, but right now you're a failure. There is no excuse, really, for missing the most important parts of life. If you regularly save lives or protect the public, then you're not a failure- you're heroic and we praise you and salute you and your sacrifices. However, if you make the best cupcakes in the state, but you're so busy that you never tuck your children in at night, then, again, I apologize, but you're a failure. But don't stop reading because I just insulted you. I want to help you grow your life by teaching you how to live an easier one.

How It All Began

My life has revolved around customer service. I began my working life as a waiter, busboy, host, and bartender at Chi-Chi's Mexican Restaurant on Staten Island, New York. I worked there from age 15 to 19. I was well suited to that life because I work hard and have an easy smile for everyone. While I attended Manhattan School of Music, I worked at Tavern On the Green in Manhattan's Central Park as a host and then as a server at Lucky's Bar and Grill on 6th Avenue. When I attended St. John's College in Annapolis, Maryland, I worked at a fine dining restaurant there. All of those restaurant jobs taught me one main lesson- teach your customer always. At Lucky's, they taught me about describing the notes of the wine, the vintage, and how to pair the wines with the menu. At the fine dining establishment in Annapolis, the Rustic Inn, I learned to memorize the ingredients of every dish, as well as the specials of the day. Every work day at Lucky's began with the manager stating in a thick New York accent, "You gotta sell, sell, sell. It's a dog-eat-dog world out there." His wine classes brought us even greater tips because we were knowledgeable about the menu and were capable of selling more wine. In Annapolis, I won the monthly wine selling contests often because I had a great memory for the wine selections and the menu. The result is that I added value to diners' experiences. When I asked the customer, "Would you like our Baked Alaska which has a premium pound cake baked in a 350 degree double boiler, filled with premium ice cream, and set aflame with Bourbon and Grand Marnier?" no one was able to say, "No, just the check." Then, when I would sing, Some Enchanted Evening, while I set the cake on fire, I knew that they would request me the next time that they dined there. Businesses need to constantly educate their customers, which will win loyalty.

After years of studying to become a classical singer at Manhattan School of Music, and then studying Mathematics and Philosophy at St. John's College, I embarked on my studies to become a Cantor and was awarded a Masters of Sacred Music and diploma of Hazzan (Cantor) in 1999 at The Jewish Theological Seminary of America. For 15 years, I worked 60-80 hours each week as a full-time Cantor for various synagogues in New York, New Jersey, Illinois, and Michigan. Eventually, although I loved the life of inspiring my fellow Jews to communicate with G-d, the politics of synagogue life proved to be extremely frustrating. After losing my job due to some synagogue politics in Michigan, I said to myself, "Life is short. It's time to do something that's going to bring a big smile to my face every morning." That smile came from opening Chazzano Coffee Roasters.

At first, there were a few months of "Woe is me, I'm losing my identity (as a clergy person), and I'm a failure." Luckily, my wife doesn't put up with my whining or minor depressive moments well. She just instructs me to get up, grow up, and deal with it. We dealt with it. We started Chazzano Coffee Roasters in earnest, and at the same time, we started our own synagogue, Hava Nashira, out of our house in Farmington Hills, MI so that we would have a place to pray with a Jewish quorum (minyan). We convened a meeting of the members of the synagogue together to discuss various issues. I charged the small community with the task of growing the synagogue by inviting their friends to attend our lovely service. The synagogue lasted for a few years, but it's almost harder to grow a small community synagogue into a vibrant volunteer-rich establishment than it is a small for-profit business. In truth, we were failures at growing the synagogue because we didn't teach our small core group how to share their love for our synagogue community with other friends and strangers. Most of the members said, But all of you are my only friends. Who else would I tell? They weren't talking to strangers at their kids' ball games, within their homeschooling network, or in line at the supermarket. They didn't know how to tell great stories about how the synagogue changed their life. To a large degree, this was because Lisa and I didn't teach our congregants (friends) how to be salespeople for the congregation. We didn't accentuate the value of what we were doing- conducting services that were small, warm, and full of education and spiritual renewal. Therefore, eventually the synagogue closed because we just couldn't consistently achieve that level of quorum that is necessary to chant all of the prayers in a traditional synagogue service.

My life in business has taught me how I could have prevented the fall of the synagogue out of my house. These same friends have referred our coffee to their friends, family, and their business colleagues. They have sent our coffee throughout the country. My friends, who regularly attended my synagogue, were more passionate about the coffee than about religious services. It was all about education and modeling. I shared my passion for coffee more, I believe, than my passion for Judaism. At that time, there was great bitterness in my soul for the synagogue and the politics of the synagogue. I was still healing, so I wasn't able to model effectively. But G-d forbid you put sugar in your coffee, and before I said anything, another person would say at the synagogue lunch, "Do you know what happens when you put sugar in Chazzano coffee?" They were my Chazzano salespeople, but not educated enough to be our small synagogue's salespeople. Sad, but true.

We then began to search for a new spiritual home and we found Congregation Beth Shalom in Oak Park, Michigan. We felt welcome and there was a vibrancy there that brought hope to our lives. So, after a few years without a regular pulpit in a synagogue, I was hired as a part-time Cantor while I worked as a full-time owner of a rapidly growing business. My journey had taken me from restaurant employee to Cantor to the coffee business and back to Cantor. This is when I began to see the parallels between a successful business and a successful spiritual community. My experience is with synagogue communities so please forgive me if I don't say church or houses of worship. They are included in this conversation. I began to see ways that my knowledge of customer service and education in the business world informed me about synagogue life and how synagogue life informed me about business.

How A Small Business Compares to A House of Worship

If you walk into Chazzano Cafe, we greet you immediately and may accost you with three different people saying, "Hello. I'll be right with you." It's almost magical- once you break that imaginary plane and place a foot into the cafe, it's important to us that you are acknowledged whether we're slammed or you're the only customer. What is implicit in the greeting is a high wattage smile that shows that we're happy that you've decided to frequent the establishment. Unsuccessful businesses or places that I'll never set foot into a second time do not have smiling employees. In those businesses, the hostess doesn't even look at you, and may even seem like you're annoying her that you came in. I often frequent the businesses that serve my coffee and find that many of them have lousy customer service. If they forget who I am and greet me with a frown, I'll just smile genuinely and say, "Hello, could you please say hello to the owner? Tell him that Frank from Chazzano is here." They usually smile and change their attitude (for me) and usher us quickly to a table. But how many people have they alienated by their behavior? Now let's look at the way in which many synagogues welcome newcomers.

The first time that I walked into a synagogue in Flushing, Queens, the very old man at the desk said to me, brusquely with a frown, "You need to put a yarmulke on in the synagogue." I happened to be wearing a yarmulke, in fact, but it was sitting a bit beyond his view. The old man could have said, "Hello. Great to see you. Are you wearing a yarmulke?" but there was no love in his voice. What if I was a prospective congregant moving to the area with my family? I would not set foot again in that synagogue. However, I was the Cantor at that synagogue for two years during school, and that was my first impression of the place, and I never forgot it.

We attended synagogue in Hamburg, Germany on a Friday night at a Chabad (Orthodox) synagogue, and no one greeted us with a "Shabbat Shalom (Peaceful Sabbath Day)." There were no smiles, no greetings of hello or goodbye. It was as if we were a nuisance. It was traumatic to even walk into a synagogue located in a country that just 75 years earlier had been the epicenter for the Holocaust; a time when Jews were sent to their death just for being Jewish. When we returned for Saturday morning services, their demeanor changed- they asked me to participate in the service, they were smiling, they engaged us in conversation, but why couldn't that have been the first impression? If I wasn't Cantor Frank, a professional clergy person who needed a place to go to synagogue on the Sabbath, they would have lost me forever.

When I was a cantor in New Jersey, my rabbi in the synagogue would walk by congregants without saying hello or engaging in small talk, then ask me a question, receive the answer, and then walk away from congregants without saying goodbye. In fact, Lisa and I have attended services in so many synagogues that were completely unfriendly that when we find a community that welcomes us and greets us warmly, we are actually surprised.

Worship communities complain that very few people attend services or become members of their church or synagogue. Do we wonder why? I don't. The prospective member often doesn't feel welcome. They aren't educated about what is happening in the synagogue, the structure of services, and the value of attending regularly. They are not greeted warmly or worse yet, they are ignored entirely. If your business treats people like that, it won't survive. So, this book will also help you grow your synagogue or church if you choose to apply its principles there. But you can also grow your son's little league organization, or your local rotary club, or your chamber of commerce.

Don't get me wrong-some of our synagogue experiences have been positive. At a synagogue in St. Louis, the entire clergy staff who were leading services had smiles on their face and in their eyes during the entire service. Again, they welcomed us into the sanctuary because they knew who I was, but there was a feeling that they were friendly to everyone. In fact, many people said hello regardless of their stature in the community. The synagogue clergy even provided us with a tour of the synagogue. The most important thing that we witnessed is that everyone participating on the bima (stage) had love in their voices. They loved what they were doing-chanting, smiling, talking about G-d's laws and teachings. Their love for G-d and G-d's people was in their voices, in their smiles, and in their actions.

When you own a business like a coffee roasterie or cafe, you don't care whether one customer smokes pot all day long, or another has more money than you will ever have, or the next customer is on food stamps but wants something that brings joy to his life. Some customers come dressed in suits and some are so scantily clad that I need to avert my eyes. I'd rather not know if they are abusive or criminals, but from the time that they walk through our doors and then walk out, we love them. We've had a chance to change their lives, to enrich their being, and perhaps make some money to support ourselves and our employees at the same time. We do not care about anything but how we can bring some joy to their lives with a great cup of coffee or tea. Now, let's turn towards your house of worship. Do you accept everyone who walks into your synagogue or church regardless of your initial judgment of them? You should. There are countless good reasons why they walked into your church or synagogue. They are seeking something, anything. Would it hurt if you came by and put your arms around them (figuratively) and said, "How may we help you? What can we do for you?" Why is that the first question that is heard at a good business but hardly ever at a house of worship?

Throughout my cantorial career, congregants have often approached me with tears in their eyes stating, "You were the only one who would say hello to me." Or synagogue leadership has said to me, "We need you here. You're the only friendly one on the clergy staff."

I often think after I speak with another business owner on the phone, "That guy has no love in his voice." Not only is he worrying about payroll, maybe he knows that someone is stealing from him, and things are just not going well, but he's lost something very important- the love for what he's doing. That passion that told him to invest his life savings, has died. I see it often. I sometimes see it as dead eyes- there's no love behind the words they speak. Have you heard a sermon from your clergy person, and said to yourself, "He has no love in his voice?" It's not that they are boring or bad speakers. They're boring or bad speakers because they lost their passion for the word of G-d. Face it; you don't get bored by someone who is passionate about a subject. If they have love or passion in their voices, they'll draw you in- you'll want to know what they're talking about regardless of your affinity for the subject. That loss of love is what happens to people who lose their passion for the career to which they have devoted themselves.

Every synagogue at which I served as Cantor, my family was always the last to leave the synagogue. I have bruises from the years that my wife or children have poked me with the signal, "Could we PLEASE leave now?" I always ignored them, as they expected me to do, because I implicitly knew that the last impression is also important. What kind of signal does it send to congregants or prospective congregants when I leave quickly after services and don't find out how we can help them?

Chazzano Coffee Roasters has been successful in gaining many wholesale accounts because I talk with businesses about the last impression: the last taste on their customers' mouths. When you dine at a lovely restaurant where you received great service and great food, and the last thing on your lips is bad, stale coffee, what will you think of that establishment? You just spent $50 per person and they couldn't manage to serve a decent cup of coffee? Now think of a house of worship where you feel very welcome and you participate in a meaningful and lovely service but the rabbi or priest doesn't greet you as you leave or doesn't speak even briefly to you after services.

In fact, it's part of Jewish tradition to run or walk quickly to synagogue and to take your time leaving for home. In that way, you are teaching people that you can't wait to join in prayer and greet the community, and that upon leaving you are reluctant to leave God's presence and you enjoyed your time at synagogue tremendously. What do you think of colleagues who clock out exactly at 5:00 p.m. every day?

There is a reason that happy business owners don't close their doors exactly at closing time. It isn't about making more money, and it is not necessarily a conscious choice. Rather, they like their shop and are not in a hurry to leave. Are you angry or frustrated when your business is flooded with customers at closing time? Embrace your customers with a great smile and enjoy their passion for your product or services. Your customers are not respecting that closing time because they feel comfortable at the business and they want to spend more time there. How cool is it that your customers love your product so much that they rushed to get to your shop before closing time? How cool is it that they knock on the door, asking or begging to buy a bag of your coffee for their breakfast? There are few accomplishments that are as rewarding as the knowledge that your product is loved and cherished. How many congregants rush to their house of worship because they don't want to be late for a particular part of the service or for the preacher's sermon? Wouldn't it be exciting if your congregants apologized profusely for being late to services? If they do, they see the value of the religious experience.

Any good salesperson knows that the first and last impressions are equally important. The last impression often includes the closing. For example, you impress your prospective client with your product and you're able to demonstrate how your product will solve their problems that you eloquently and accurately described. If they are ready to close the deal, but then you say, "Oh, we can't fulfill this order for another few months from now." Or, "I'll call you tomorrow and we'll finalize the deal." But you forget to call until three days later and your last impression just killed the deal. Have you ever dined at a great restaurant, and you're flying high with delight as you realize that you found a great new place, and then you excuse yourself to go to the bathroom? You discover the bathroom has a terrible odor and the garbage can has not been emptied for hours and it's overflowing onto the floor. The toilets...let's not even think about them. You think, "to what else are they not paying attention?" Your favorite new restaurant now becomes a place of no return. You politely leave a nice tip, but you'll never come back. Whether you're running a business or non-profit, you need to think about every possible experience that the customer will have with the organization. The first and last impression needs to be planned out. How many times do you hear, "Great to see you," or "Thank you for coming in," or "We hope to see you soon?" Kill the customer with kindness when they walk in and when they leave. Can you sneak out of a business or house of worship without anyone saying goodbye? If yes, then they won't be able to keep you as a customer.

Interviewing Customers

We've now reached a new and useful tool: Interviewing your customer. For those of you who are nosy, interested, and concerned about total strangers, this chapter will be easy. I want to teach you how to interview strangers/customers in your daily life whether at your house of worship, business, or at your favorite specialty food store. When you attended a child's recital, did you ask everyone sitting around you what they do for a living? The person next to you on line at the supermarket may be your ticket to a better life. What's the harm in finding out whether you can help them or they can help you? Yes, you're correct. There isn't any! I'll teach you some techniques to help you grow your life and maybe recruit new people into your business or organization.

Remember you're creating a community. Strangers are talking to one another. In my case, I can introduce regular customers to a new customer who is enjoying the best cup of coffee they've ever had. "What's your name? Bob, meet Sarah. Sarah is a family lawyer. I hope that you never need her." When Bob comes in again and sees Sarah, Bob already has a stronger sense of belonging in this place he just discovered.

Then you ask Bob what he does for a living.

"Oh, you produce social media videos for businesses?"

"Great. Do you have some cards? I'm a crazy networker- I'll share your cards with my business friends."

"Hey Bob, meet a friend of mine who owns an elevator business. Tom, this is Bob who creates social media videos for business. If you need help with training videos or just instructional videos for your website, that's what Bob does."

"Bob, your coffee will be ready in a few minutes."

We just began to "interview" the customer by asking what they did for a living. We'll also ask, "what is your target market?"

Look, this is in a coffee shop, not a cancer research center, a chamber of commerce, or a political reception. Although we sell coffee by the pound or the cup, the point of the business is really to enrich our customers' lives. We want you to leave our business healthier and maybe even wealthier--than when you first entered. Sure, you'll receive the best cup of coffee in the world, but you may leave with a few thousand dollars more in your pocket because I introduced you to the right person. By the way, that social media guru rescheduled the appointment he set with me because he was shooting a video for the elevator business. Really! In addition, when my family and I went on vacation for two weeks, Sarah, that family lawyer, publicly thanked me for providing $2500 of closed business for her while I was gone. All of the people that I introduced to her eventually needed her services.

Did our new customer Bob just move to town? If so, he could probably use the business card of my favorite plumber and the best business lawyer I know. I may have just enriched Bob's personal and business life. In addition, he left with a pound of coffee because he loved that he could drink it black. He may come back tomorrow and buy some for his mother-in-law who is always complaining about bad coffee. "How's the new home in town? Have you completely moved in? Before you fully move in, if you want to enjoy a great meal, here is a list of the best restaurants in town. Tell them that Frank from Chazzano Coffee sent you."

Remember that the main goal of this book is to teach you how to balance your business and your life. Grow your business without losing what is most important--family, friends, and your health. A key way to do this is to teach your customers the value of your business so that you expend less time and energy gaining new customers. It's just referral marketing but more controlled and product/service specific. When you interview your customer, they will purchase services or product from you first. They will remember that you cared about their lives.

If you educate your customer, they will teach and educate their friends and family about your business, and eventually become your unpaid sales team. You've enriched their life and they want to help you grow your business so that you remain a force in their lives.

When I tell my children where I'm going, I often say, I'm going to the coffee "shul" (synagogue). This flub has many connotations of meaning. "Shul", which is used by many Jews to refer to the synagogue, really means "school." My business is a school, accidentally and purposefully. At the cafe, I teach networking, social media skills, and customer service to all of my business friends and customers. The Chamber of Commerce often sends new members or new business owners to my cafe, because Chazzano Coffee is a place to learn about business. My time is filled with impromptu mini sermons about how to grow your business or life.

If you translate "shul" as synagogue, the true meaning of the word is "meeting place". The Hebrew word for synagogue is "Beit K'nesset" or house of meeting. Chazzano Coffee is a place of meeting. We created an environment where you can grow your business just by sitting and sipping a great cup of coffee. Throughout the day, I introduce business owners who have a synergy and I try to obtain closed business for them. Remember the lawyer friend who closed $2500 worth of business through the cafe when I was on vacation? It consisted of third tier referrals--I introduced her to someone who then introduced someone else to her who then introduced someone else to her.

If you sit at the bar for a while, as people come up to the bar to order, we'll say,

"Do you know each other? Let me introduce you!"

As the two strangers speak, we brew their coffee or tea, and assist with the conversation. When we occasionally hear, "Are you Bob? I haven't seen you since high school! You're a regular Chazzano customer, too?" we know that we've created a community that helps our customers grow their lives.

I've done well at BNI, Business Networking International, an awesome referral marketing business group with chapters around the world. Chazzano Coffee has grossed over $300K of closed business because of referrals and warm introductions given to me from BNI chapter members. When I started Chazzano Coffee full-time in 2009, I knew few business owners. When we opened Chazzano Cafe in Ferndale, Michigan in October 2009, I realized that I now had a wonderful opportunity to share referrals and provide warm introductions to my business friends. I collected all of my customers' business cards, and I frequently walk other customers and business friends to the large table filled with business cards. If they own their own business, I ask, "Do you have a great business lawyer, a great graphic designer, or a great commercial insurance agent? I trust these people. Give them a call." If you own your own business, I want you to use your good power to help others grow their businesses. Our cafe has been called the mini-BNI because we help people grow their businesses and provide networking opportunities. If you have good power to change the world, use it.

To add to the synagogue theme of Chazzano, and without sounding crazy and full of hubris, the cafe has the feeling of a house of peace and serenity. Houses of worship generally are sanctuaries away from the busy world. You pray to the Divine to take yourself away from the regular, loud world, and try to bring serenity to your life. Customers use the cafe to write books, or just stare out the window and decompress from the troubles of the world. It's part of what makes one a good host-knowing what your guest desires and making them as comfortable as possible.

So, how do you make your business into a house of worship? You interview your customers. Interviewing is not just for filling a position in your company or for getting a job, it's a way of life. Spend time asking what they're doing during the weekend.

"Anything exciting happening during the weekend?"

"Anything exciting happening today?"

"No, just work."

"What do you do for work?"

When I know what a regular customer does for a living, we will ask, "How's work?"

"It's work."

"What would you love to do?"

If I know that your dream is to become a fine furniture artist, I'll connect you with other woodworking artists. If an artist comes in to the cafe after you've left, I'll connect you both while I still remember our conversation. I connect people that can help each other, because when you have great power to do good in the world, you are obligated to use that power as often as possible.

Be a pastoral presence in your business. In Judaism, it's a commandment to ask people how their spouses, children, significant others are feeling. It's a commandment to care about other human beings as if you are the clergy of your business. Regardless of your reasons, noble or financial, people love you when you care about them. If they like you, they will want to buy from you. They'll rejoice as they see you grow. Then, when you ask, "Mary, how's the new baby?," they'll love you even more. You remembered their name and what is happening in their lives.

Here's how I interview prospective Chazzano employees. I schedule an appointment with them for a certain time- let's say, 10:00 a.m. They arrive, if they're smart, by 9:45. My employees notify me that they are present. I tell my employee, "I'll be right there." I come by to their seat at 10:00 a.m., say hello, introduce myself, and then I tell them I'll be right back. I spend about 10 minutes more answering e-mails, making phone calls, all the while watching them to see if they interact with other people in the cafe. Are they smiling? Are they talking to complete strangers? Are they asking my employees questions about the shop or coffee? Are they serial interviewers like I am? If they don't have crazy good interpersonal skills, they are not the right fit for my team. However, beyond all of the questions about their previous employment, I ask them, "What was your favorite job?" "What was your least favorite job?" And here are the most important questions: "What do you want to be when you grow up? What is your dream job? If you were wealthy, how would you spend your days?"

These are the questions that you should ask everyone that you meet, eventually. They may be doing X job, but how wonderful would it be if you helped them find Y job which also happens to be their dream right now? If you know what they truly want to do, wouldn't it be great and fortuitous if your next client/customer actually was looking for someone to fill a position that was their Y job?

The local job seekers are told to come see me. I ask them pointed questions: "Sure, that's what you were doing for 10 years, but do you really want to get another job like that?" "What do you really want to do? Send me your resume, and I'll send it to some business friends who may be looking for you."

There are a multitude of businesses that sell coffee, or provide plumbing services, or heating and cooling, or fix garage doors. However, if you want your customers to remember you, help improve their lives beyond the services that you offer. Interview them and truly get to know them. They'll refer you, their garage door repairman, to their neighbors when you improve their lives by recommending your favorite trusted landscaper or dentist to them. Who else does that?

Houses of worship must also interview you about your religious and personal/business lives. In addition, they should provide business counseling in addition to spiritual counseling. I cannot tell you how many poorly written "membership packets" I had to fill out when I became one of the clergy leaders in each community I served. The intake forms were almost always copied poorly, with spelling errors and unintelligble questions. No one should be interviewed by filling out badly constructed membership packets. In addition, many of the questions are those that the average congregant cannot answer without feeling idiotic. Instead of asking you questions, face to face, and assisting you with the form, you are faced with questions about your knowledge of Jewish practices and what is your Hebrew name. All of those questions are important, but it's just as important to get to know what each member does for a living, what their target market is, and what brings them joy in their lives. Do they send their kids to a certain camp during the summer? Do they work crazy late shift hours of 7pm to 7am every day? Why are they joining the house of worship? There are so many other synagogues or churches around the area. Why did you choose this one? How may we help your family feel welcome in our community?

We need to interview them about what really makes them special. This membership introduction to the synagogue can create possibilities that allow the congregation to thrive financially and spiritually. If the synagogue leadership finds ways for this new family to grow financially, won't this family make sure that the synagogue in turn grows financially? Do you know what I want to see at all houses of worship? Networking groups of all kinds! Business networking, homeschooling networking, Jewish Day School networking, women who have just had a new baby networking, even people who have just lost their jobs networking. Make the house of worship a place to assist in communication with G-d, but make sure that it touches all parts of our lives.

When a new customer visits Chazzano Coffee Roasters, we ask them how they heard about us. It's important to ask that simple question because you need to know where your most effective marketing and branding is occurring. If most or many customers are coming from one or two sources, I'm sure you're going to pour more resources into those places. Synagogues need to be sure to ask, "Where did you hear about us? Of all of the synagogues in the area, why did you join ours?"

Above all, the lesson is to be kind to everyone. Listen to what they have to say about their lives. But, don't let them suck the life out of you. I tell my business friends, prospective wholesale customers, and job seekers to "use me." Use my network, my knowledge about sales and marketing, and use me as a sounding board for your life. Ivan Misner, the father of referral marketing, wrote a book called *Giver's Gain*. You gain if you spend your life giving. All of those people for whom you provided encouragement or helped secure a job will never forget you. In fact, they'll always remember you and they will want to give back. It's never expected, but it's always appreciated.

Do you know what the highest act of kindness--or highest level of commandment--is in Judaism? It's burying the dead. Why? The dead cannot repay you. We naturally help others who can also help us in return, but what a beautiful world we could live in if everyone helped others regardless of their ability to be repaid. The highest act of kindness according to a famous 12th century Rabbi, Moses Maimonides, is to provide someone with a job without that person knowing who helped them get it.

Your kindness to others will lead to ways for them to help you in your life. They'll find ways for you to grow your life and business. Stick your neck out always for others. You will be rewarded with a great life. The truth is that you never know where you're going career-wise. I used to believe that I would be a full-time synagogue Cantor until I died. It may still happen, but it's doubtful now. Right now, I'm an entrepreneur with a passion for business and coffee, but is that all I am? What is the next chapter in my life? My life seems to be circular, Cantor to businessman to Cantor/businessman. I have no idea whether my life will be a holding pattern until I retire. I surely hope not- I have more dreams to realize.

Educated Customers are Loyal Customers

For those not of the Jewish faith, synagogue services are complex, daunting and confusing. In a conservative or orthodox synagogue, one needs to know to put a head covering on and a prayer shawl over your shoulders. The prayer book is mainly in Hebrew with English translation, but the prayers are always chanted completely in Hebrew. When you walk into the synagogue, the greeters expect that you know which book to pick up and use, and how to read and follow along during the service. Furthermore, imagine having a doctorate in some area of study and then feeling incredibly stupid in your own synagogue. Then imagine forcing yourself to sit in synagogue, hearing beautiful singing for three hours.

It sounds like torture to me- and I'm a professional Jewish clergyperson.

I remember the first time that I was invited to Lisa's home for Passover. My mother was Jewish and my father was Italian Catholic which meant that I was automatically Jewish by birth. However, beyond my mother saying to me when she was angry with my father, "Frankie, remember that you're a Jew," I had no formal religious upbringing. I remember sitting for 4 hours while Lisa's family sang beautiful songs in Hebrew, read in Hebrew, and had heated discussions about certain Hebrew words. At that point in my life, I had learned to speak Russian, Italian, French, German and learned to read and translate Ancient Greek. However, I didn't know a letter of Hebrew! I felt like an idiot. Her parents thought that I was some sweet dope from Staten Island who wasn't that bright. I said to myself, "That's it! I'm going to be fluent in the prayers by next year!" I asked Lisa to make a cassette tape of all of the music of the service. I began to study Hebrew with a college professor at St. John's College. In three months, I was able to lead the service if I was asked and my Hebrew reading was now fluent. It's likely you're not as competitive as I am- so I'm a bad role model. I was in love with a brilliant, observant Jew, I wanted to be accepted in the family, and of course, I wanted them to know that I, too, was brilliant. But most people aren't as driven as I am. I had an ulterior motive to become knowledgeable about my faith. But how do you educate members of your faith who are lost and feel lonely in a crowd?

There's another point about Passover seders at Lisa's home. They were absolutely joyous. Do you know how to educate anyone with greater ease? Show them that you love what you are doing. Lisa and her family were singing, smiling, and joking around. There was infectious laughter. Funerals and death beds are not truly joyous, but besides those two examples, everything should be shared with gladness. I was infected by the joy of Lisa's family.

Do you know what other experience brought me closer to Judaism and the life of Jewish clergy? In Annapolis, I attended St. John's College, almost immediately after I left Manhattan School of Music. While in Annapolis, Maryland, and with the renewed love of Judaism received from Lisa's family, I began attending Shabbat morning services at the local Orthodox synagogue. I truly knew nothing except that I loved the music of the synagogue and I loved being a Jew. The Cantor at this synagogue had a voice from G-d. When I describe it, tears begin collecting quickly. That was one entry point for my renewed love of Judaism. The Cantor befriended me and gave me a few cassette tape recordings of some simpler services for me to learn. However, the young rabbi at the congregation is the one who I will always remember. In Orthodox and Conservative religious services, there are certain prayers during which one is not permitted to speak. They are moments of meditation and deep communication with G-d. However, as always, I had a million questions. He, the rabbi of the congregation, always answered them. If I ever met him again, I'm sure he wouldn't remember those moments. However, he sat with me patiently, answered questions, and taught me about the value of the experience. Do we take enough time to do this in our businesses? How can we transform complete strangers into customers or congregants who feel ownership of our organizations?

Cash flow can be rough for small companies as well as very large companies. At one point in Chazzano's existence, I said, Enough! My wholesale accounts were paying me when they wanted, or could, pay me. My cash flow was erratic and mostly non-existent and Chazzano wasn't making enough to justify its existence. I put my foot down and gently asked everyone to pay COD or net 15 at most. Several months later, a large account changed the payment terms from COD to net 15 or net 30 depending on their cash flow. I emailed the owner and asked him to reconsider. He declined and stated, "Let me know how you want to proceed," which means, "Take it or Leave it." I then asked him to call me that day. He answered quickly, "I'm booked all day long." I then chose to burn a bridge, for there are some bridges that deserve to be burned. I wrote back, "I know that no matter how big Chazzano Coffee becomes, I will never tell a small business owner that I'm too busy to talk to them." It's true. I will even tell annoying telemarketers why I am not even going to listen to their elevator speech before I hang up. The reason? I have local business friends who are helping me with that particular service. When daily deal coupon companies call, I often give them advice on how to get more business from companies that need their service. Talk to everyone. Learn from everyone. Greet everyone with a smile. Have a smile in your voice, always. Educate your customers and your vendors, always.

Coffee Is Coffee, Right?

Not really. Couldn't be less true, actually. Which coffee would you like? We have over 25 different single origin coffees. My favorite is this one- Ethiopia Harrar. It has notes of blueberry, cherry, pipe tobacco, and a red wine finish. I joke around: "It's what G-d drinks because it's so complex." In just a few sentences, I have either impressed you with my lunacy (passion) about coffee, or turned you off because I'm not only a lunatic but I'm a coffee snob and no one likes a coffee snob, unless they're one themselves. Or, just maybe, I've helped bring you out of your everyday life and lifted the veil about coffee. In mere moments, you've become more knowledgeable about coffee than most of the world. Beyond all of that, I've brought you into the fold of our magical business. It's not just a coffee business. Nor is it just a cafe. There's something special.

All coffee originates from the area around Ethiopia and Uganda. The song is correct that "There's an awful lot of coffee in Brazil," but coffee was eventually planted in Brazil hundreds of years after coffee began to be used as a beverage. Did you know that in Papua New Guinea (Indonesia) coffee was first planted in 1954? It's one of the most popular coffees in the world but it's a very new crop. Then if I add that Papua New Guinea used to be our most popular on-line seller, have I hooked you in yet? What happens if I then tell you that the Papua New Guinea coffee that we have has notes of peaches and chocolate? Are you interested in at least trying some? I'm sure that you will. With all of the information that I've shared with you about the coffee, I am adding more and more layers to the value of the coffee. When you dine at a restaurant where the waiter carefully enunciates every ingredient in the entree selections, or shares with you their favorite wines and their flavor profiles, aren't you feeling blessed that you are able to make such an informed decision about your experience? The food at other restaurants may be better designed or prepared, but are they more valuable to your life? Does the experience enrich your life? If not, save your money and eat cheaply at home.

I've told you about the coffee that G-d drinks, Ethiopia Harrar, but have I discussed the coffee that the angels drink? The answer is the angels drink Yemen Mocca Sanani. Why? It is the most extraordinary coffee that you'll ever drink- it has notes of pepper and chocolate, like a Mexican hot chocolate.

A shot of Yemen Mocca Sanani as an espresso is exquisite. The question that my staff and I had was how do we price the Yemen coffee? It's worth $45/lb. but that's too much for our customers and we wanted more people to be able to purchase this phenomenal coffee. The beginning private discussion began with $26/lb., but that seemed underpriced The simple reason that we felt that $26 was too low, was the extraordinary education and added value that we gave to this coffee. It is legendary at Chazzano Coffee Roasters. People constantly ask us, "Will you ever get the Yemen back? That has to be my favorite coffee, ever!" (I blogged about how difficult it is to get the Yemen coffee into the United States due to civil war there.) In addition, it's related to the coffee that G-d drinks- it was taken from Ethiopia Harrar and planted in Yemen during the 9th century. The coffee is expensive for us to purchase and the last time that we received a lot from Yemen was two years ago. For all of those reasons, we priced the Yemen at $36/pound. Guess how long it took to sell 105 pounds of Yemen Mocca Sanani? Only 2 weeks.

There are four things lacking in most houses of worship:

1-Lack of Enthusiasm

2-Lack of New Visitors

3-Lack of Follow Through

4-Lack of Integrity

Looking Inside Yourself For Direction

The first lack: Enthusiasm

I believe that it's time for some introspection about your feelings about your house of worship. Ask yourself this: How many of your synagogues' membership are so crazy in love with the synagogue that they go on and on about how great a synagogue event or service is to them? How many people speak with excitement about what they learned at your church? Yes, there are many people who love their pastor or rabbi, but why aren't they coming to church or synagogue every Sabbath?

Why do I join fitness centers and pay a monthly bill to NOT work out? I have spent thousands of dollars on membership at different gyms for decades. In the beginning, I work out several times each week. However, I often found a reason to do something else. I was too tired. I had too much work to do. The reason that I joined the gym at first is that I felt obligated to work out, to improve my physical fitness, to feel better about my appearance. However, a few visits in my new membership, no one knows who I am. They aren't asking me, "What are your goals?" When I walk in each time, they don't ask me how I'm doing. They take my ID card, swipe it, and without looking at me, say: "Have a nice workout." I have great self-esteem, but I expect any business that I frequent to know my name and say hello to me with a huge smile.

There are many ways to add enthusiasm to a congregant's experience. What if you brought a newcomer up to the ark and pointed out the history of each Torah scroll? (This was dedicated by Saul and Roberta Schwartz who love the community and came to services every Saturday...) During the service, tell the newcomer something exciting to you about what's going on at any given time. If they're synagogue novices, kill them with cool knowledge about the service. (Hey, here are the Rabbi and Cantor's seats, but what is cooler is this area behind the scenes where the Rabbi and Cantor prepare for the services and maybe even have a private stash of snacks or soda.) They'll say to themselves, "This is unique. I knew nothing but I felt at home." The newcomer has a sense of ownership. In a few hours, they've been enriched with knowledge or just camaraderie.

Have you hired clergy and elected lay leaders who speak with joy in their eyes about the synagogue? Are they smiling so much that you think that there might me something wrong with them? Does the rabbi or cantor sound giddy when they share something that they just learned? Do they sound like a kid who just learned how to properly pronounce a word that they've been reading to themselves incorrectly? If the priest sounds spiritless about the subject, they've lost the love and excitement concerning their learning.

Listen to your favorite annoying "inspirational" speaker. I say annoying because they are exactly what businesses and houses of worship need. They are over excited about the topic. One of my favorite speakers is Joel Osteen. I know that I'm incorrect, but he smiles so much that I think that there's something wrong with him. He is so completely passionate about everything he says that it's infectious. He was the son of a preacher, and now he's a well-known preacher himself. He is thrilled about everything that he teaches. At least, that's the way his sermons and books sound, positively joyous. Everything that your leaders teach must have this same level of excitement. Why would I go to a class when the person announcing it has no joy in their voice? Have you seen the famous scene in the movie Ferris Bueller's Day Off, where the teacher drones on, "Bueller? Bueller?" Why do we remember so few awesome teachers in our lifetime? The teachers that I remember had a sparkle in their eyes.

If someone asked us at Chazzano, "how is this coffee?" and we said, "fine," would you buy it? But if we said with a smile, gushing, "It's my favorite coffee of all the coffee selections," you'd probably buy a few pounds. When we ask a customer, "How's the coffee?" They often say, "Awesome!" or "Fantastic!" or some other joyous description. Occasionally, we'll hear, "Good" or "Fine." To which I might respond, "Just fine?" or "Just good? Let me get you an awesome cup of coffee." Education without a smile is useless.

Put the joy back into worship. This is not about singing songs in a major key or clapping hands while we dance around the sanctuary. Those tricks get old and they're not for everyone. However, trace a smile from beginning to end of the service. Bring enthusiasm into greeting people and end services with enthusiastic announcements. If your leaders can't find their enthusiasm, find new leaders. When someone in your employ is poisoning the spirits of other employees, it's time to fire them before the others get infected. If your synagogue President frowns all the time, your synagogue is in trouble. The President doesn't even like the community of which he is an integral part. One of my favorite sayings is, "The fish rots from the head down." If there is a problem with the business or house of worship, look at the leaders. It's their fault. Equally, if you see a healthy business or house of worship, look at the leaders of those institutions. The greatness of the institution comes from their leadership.

A famous Rabbi of ancient times would say, "When you teach a child, it's as if you've given birth to them." Do you have friends who share tidbits of information that, at first, you really don't care about? I love and adore my son, Max, but sometimes he'll share something completely foreign to me about computers. I love that he's passionate about the subject, but I have no idea what he's talking about when he talks about Java, html, GUI (graphical user interface), xml, and many other topics. But Max, and your passionate but annoying friends, are enriching our lives. They are bringing you to greater heights with their knowledge. You're learning about things that you never believed would matter. That issue that your mechanic is discussing with you for 20 minutes is helping you grow your life. The first time that I used graphical user interface in a sentence correctly was a beautiful moment. Then when I learned that I should just say, User Interface, because everything is really graphical these days? My son's enthusiasm for the subject enriched my life even more.

When you educate your customer, you're bringing them peace, comfort and ownership. You're helping them grow and learn. You're creating long term relationships with them that will help you grow your business. They'll tell their friends about the guy who is so passionate about his business. Your customer will now help you grow your business and become a passionate part of your unpaid sales force. This all happened because you educated them about your business and helped grow their life. Now, they're returning the favor and helping to grow your life. Imagine if you created other happy, enriched customers who sing your praises. That means less work in growing your business, more time with your family, and more balance to your life.

With regard to houses of worship, if you find ways to enthusiastically educate your members, you won't have to spend so much time trying to retain them or discussing why membership numbers are down. You'll have more time to spend with your family because you won't be constantly putting out fires.

Here is a fictional letter to the President of a fictional synagogue:

Dear Ms. President,

Wow, what an awesome experience I had this weekend. A friend of mine from your board told me how great this place is. Now I know how correct she is in her judgment. First, I walked into the synagogue, and 7 people greeted me warmly with "Shabbat Shalom." They seemed to go out of their way to say hello-- Then I was happily approached by half a dozen people who stopped their conversations, turned toward me and said "Good Shabbes, Welcome." I was so impressed with the friendliness- everyone had a smile on their faces like they were happy to be there.

Then I entered the beautiful sanctuary- the greeter, I don't know what he's called, greeted me with a smile and asked me if I was visiting and who'd invited me. He then introduced me to your visitor hosts who offered to sit with me and make sure I knew where we were in the service.

The service was lovely- it reminded me of my services growing up- the Cantor had a lovely voice- he looked like he was having a great time- The Rabbi and Cantor were smiling broadly when they spoke with each other. They seemed to be friends.

What I found astonishing and outstanding is that the Rabbi, before his sermon, asked the visitors, and there were many, to stand. The Rabbi asked us to tell the congregation our name, where we're from, why we were there, and what we wanted to get out of the experience. It was wonderful because it made me feel welcome and it felt like they were interviewing me.

I loved all of the kids playing-sometimes quietly, sometimes not so quietly-around the sanctuary. No one shushed them once. There was a lot of singing throughout the service and the congregation seemed to enjoy singing along.

I appreciated how you asked us gently at the Kiddush whether we were interested in being partners in the congregation and you introduced us to your membership chairperson who shared the reasons why he loves the synagogue and community.

Thank you for succeeding in making me feel welcome in this wonderful community.

All the best,

Your newest congregant, Samantha

Whenever my contract negotiations would begin and the committee argued that the synagogue didn't have enough money to provide a proper raise, they would say, the problem is that "the synagogue should be run like a business". They were correct but for different reasons. Synagogues are different from businesses because synagogues really just need to cover costs- the clergy and staff salaries, and money for special programming, religious services, and utility and insurance costs. The financial goal of a synagogue is to break even at the end of the year and maybe have some money for a rainy day. A business must be showing increased revenue each year. Increased revenue is often the result of greater market share or more customers. Therefore, there must be another way that synagogues should be run like a business. Growing businesses educate their customers and show the value of being a "member" or customer. Healthy businesses have great customer service that extends throughout the different modes of experience that the member has with the business. Synagogues should have business-like customer service and enthusiastic education that adds value to the synagogue product or services.

Synagogues are always chasing after their members to pay their synagogue dues because they're always running out of money. When you negotiate for a raise with any company, they might say that "we can't; we just don't have the money".

However, we all know that it really isn't "I can't" it's more "I won't". The same can be said for many congregants who say they cannot pay full dues. They say "they can't" but they then go away for two weeks on vacation. It's not even that they're lying. They really "can't" because the experience of being a member of the congregation is not as valuable as that trip. They "won't" because there are so many other things that have greater value for them and their families that they "can't" pay full dues. So how do you show the value of a membership in your organization? You need to educate them. But they need to be entertained by the education.

Here are some easy ways to educate a fellow congregant in any religion:

1. When they walk into the house of worship, give them a short tour of the place. Educate them about how long you have been worshiping in this place. How long has the clergy been serving the community? Hand them a prayerbook. Tell them on what page the service starts. Give them a brief primer on what will happen in the service. Introduce them to someone who is friendly and knowledgeable about the service.

2. Don't send out badly written flyers asking people to volunteer in the synagogue. Personally ask them to accompany you to visit someone who is ill and in the hospital or at home. Teach them about how to visit the sick. Pair the

new prospective member with like-minded people to whom they are close in age. Mentor the new member.

3. The prospective member should be invited to lunch or dinner by a different congregant every week. They should be "killed with kindness". This will also expose them to different viewpoints about what the congregation has to offer.

4. The prospective member should feel like a rag doll that every child wants. No, I want to play with her. No, she's mine! (Of course, not in a creepy way.)

5.   Furthermore, if the prospective member has a business- how will you help put money in her hands? If she's a printer, send some printing work her way, or find ways for her to meet other professionals in her field of expertise.

6. Reach your customers/ congregants through their natural channels of communication. Snail mail is still great for some things, but not for modern business communication. Use social media to reach them. If they have not reached the digital age, go visit them with a care package, or call them to just say hello. Thank them for past business and wish them well.

Synagogue membership reminds me of my past gym memberships. If you own a business that depends on membership dues, your enthusiasm and joy are at their highest when you receive a new dues paying member. There will be less worries about payroll or cash flow this month!

However, after those first few weeks, our enthusiasm dies and we forget the new member as we search for other new members to join our organization. Later we lament that we couldn't keep last year's new members. If we helped them feel ownership of the place, or if we educated them about the organization, they would possibly be so enthusiastic that the new members would bring their friends to the congregation.

When people come into Chazzano cafe for the first time, they are often bewildered by the vast amount of coffee selections available. Then they're confused about the amount of different ways of brewing the coffee- French Press, Vacuum Syphon Brewer, Pourover, Turkish, Espresso, Cold Brew, and many more. Then, we may talk about how coffee has double the flavor possibilities of wine, 1500 possibilities. When we begin to discuss that the Ethiopian Harrar has notes of blueberry, cherry, pipe tobacco with a red wine finish, we have either killed a piece of their soul, or we have brought them to coffee nirvana. Regardless, after we've interviewed them about what kind of coffee they'd like and how they'd like to brew it, we ask, "Would you like a tour?" The reason that we do this is because we want them to feel like they're at home. There's one secret to our success at Chazzano Coffee Roasters. We're enthusiastic because we truly are passionate about coffee and improving our customers' lives. When you visit our cafe, the tour is enjoyable because we love what we are doing.

Have you ever stayed at someone's house who won't let you explore one of the rooms? Have you ever looked into their medicine cabinet? I haven't, but it's tempting. The only home tours that I've been given is when the square footage is huge and the homeowners own works of art that will probably make their way into a museum after their death. "Would you like a tour" is a way to give them ownership of the place and make it special for them, an approach I recommend to use with prospective members or your synagogue or church.

Networking and Sales

I am a master networker. I have received at least $300K in referrals and probably have given a like amount. I'm successful because I train my customers and business friends how to sell Chazzano coffee. I educate them how to help me grow my business. Every year since we opened four years ago, Chazzano Coffee Roasters won the Best Coffee Shop in Detroit. I needed educated and zealous customers to make that happen. I asked them for months during the various "Best of" contests to vote for us and noted how the exposure would help us grow. I would tell some referral partners and customers to share the story, "the food was great, the service was great, but the coffee was terrible. I have a friend, Frank, who has the best coffee. May I give him your contact information?" Or, I'd educate them about the fact that we give three week old coffee to homeless shelters. Or they share the joke about "G-d cries and an angel loses its wings." If I want a warm introduction to a specialty market, I remind them about the other specialty markets that carry Chazzano Coffee. The goal of any salesperson is to come to a sales call with closed business. I expect that when I meet the prospective customer, they almost immediately want to do business with me because my referral partner told them so much about my business that they just needed to meet me in person. My personal closing rate has always been around 85% because I am always teaching my customers and business friends about my business.

The Second Lack: New Visitors

So, how do you get closed business for your synagogue? How do you get visitors to see value in a synagogue membership? Treat your organization like a growing business- educate your membership in the ways to educate their friends and business colleagues about the organization. If you lack an army of salespeople, you're lost. Your business or house of worship will continue to struggle. First, teach your synagogue leaders how to share their love for the synagogue. Teach them to tell stories to their friends about a great experience they had at their synagogue. If my friend attends church every week and she never tells me about the church, I'm going to assume two things. One, she doesn't like attending the church so she wants to save me the pain of visiting. Or, two, she loves the church, but she doesn't believe that I'm worthy of being a part of the community. If you love your religious institution, tell everyone that you know about it. Invite your like-minded friends. Refer them to your church. Ask them, do you know someone else who might like to visit my church? I love being part of such a beautiful community and I want others to feel the same joy.

I mostly hear gossip about other synagogues. Did you hear about what the Cantor did? The board is really upset with the Rabbi. That other synagogue is stealing our members. It's not our fault that younger members are not attending synagogue events. Who wants to be a member of a particular synagogue when the members are bad mouthing the clergy, leadership or service?

I look forward to having a full head of gray or white hair. I will embrace my senior status in the community. However, it will still depress me to be surrounded by mainly senior citizens in synagogue, at the opera house, or at the art museum. An organization, except for AARP, that doesn't have new, younger members all of the time, will die a slow and painful death. Do you have 10 new people who inquire about your business or synagogue every week? If not, why not?

I have known several synagogues that have a serious cash flow problem in June. Why? Congregants leave to go on vacation, synagogue programs cease, and everyone is saving their money for donations during the High Holidays in

September and October. But, it happens every year! Surely someone at some point has woken up and said, "What will we do next June so this doesn't happen again?" Sadly, the definition of insanity comes to mind. You know it's when you do the same thing over and over again and expect different results. Synagogues and businesses need new members or customers all of the time. One way is to build up your sales team. How many visitors came to services in March? Not many? If you tripled the number of visitors from January to March, do you believe that the synagogue will have a cash flow problem in June? What if you taught your leaders how to educate their acquaintances about the benefits of being part of the synagogue? What if you then had enthusiastic and loving follow through? The cash flow problem in June would probably evaporate.

Selling is About Bringing People into your Community

The best salesperson is a problem solver. Before you meet your prospective client, know their particular problems or challenges and know how to solve them. When you're in your house of worship, look around. Do you see anyone who looks uncomfortable or lonely? Do some visual research. Go ahead and say hello to them and see if you can be of any help. When I see people in synagogue with frowns, those are the first people I greet. It's my personal challenge to take that frown and turn it into a smile. Make them forget their sorrow or depression for a while. Make them feel cherished. Most organizations, business or non-profits, are reactionary. Do you have membership issues? Do you have problems keeping regular customers? The problem begins with poor selling skills. Selling skills also extend to your capacity to love, ability to educate, interview and smile. Remember our home synagogue? Solve their problems before their problems become a membership issue.

Every synagogue leader that I know laments about poor membership. The board blames their Rabbi. The Rabbi blames the synagogue president. It takes a village to raise a child. It also takes a village to destroy a village. There are often debriefing meetings about who has dropped their synagogue membership. There are countless meetings about how to get new members. It is my belief that the synagogue was lucky to have them and their dues money even for a little while because the disenfranchised member was upset with the organization because of a lack of feeling part of the community. If the member was greeted warmly, educated about how to be an effective and beloved member, and was included and sought after for events, there would be no possible way that they would leave.

The last part of educating your sales team is persistence. It is also part of closing business. Here's a story about persistence. Several years ago, I was unsuccessfully trying to get a warm introduction to Whole Foods Market. Then I asked a regular customer, where do you work? He works at Whole Foods! I told him that Chazzano Coffee should be sold at Whole Foods because it's the freshest coffee around, we roast fresh to order and expect it to sell within 3 weeks. I told him that it is a perfect fit for Whole Foods' belief in fresh, healthy, and local food. He referred and recommended me to the regional coffee purchaser and suddenly it was closed business. However, six months later, then nine months later, Chazzano Coffee still wasn't on the shelves. During those long months, I sent e-mails every week to see if I could speed the process along. I kept in touch and secured the continued confidence that Chazzano would be sold at Whole Foods Market. Finally, about a year later, the coffee was on the shelves and sold well. It took another specialty market in Michigan over six months after a successful sales call to place Chazzano Coffee on the shelves as well. I called the VP every month to just say hello. Finally, there was a restaurant owner who loved our coffee, but when I called every week, they'd say, "Frank, we love your coffee, but we're really busy this week, call us next week." They did that to us for eight months until I said, "If you're not interested, that's not a problem, I still love your restaurant, but I'll stop calling you about Chazzano Coffee." The restaurateur said, "Frank, are you available to meet on Thursday?" When you're unmarried and unattached and you really like someone, it often takes persistence to get that first or second date. Persistence, (not stalking), reminds people that you find their business or membership important.

Creating Amnesia of Happiness

From our grand opening in October 2009 until today, we have received constant phone calls from people who are embarrassed because they left the cafe and forgot to pay! This happens to regulars as well as to new customers. It's really our fault. We made them feel so comfortable that they forgot that it was a business transaction. They came in to get a small coffee. Simple, right? Not really. We may have asked them, "What's new?" or "What are you doing today?" or "How's business?" or "Are you doing anything fun today?" That changes the scenery from a coffee shop to your friend's house or maybe your church. How often do you learn about the people closest to you when you ask, "What's new?" Often, Lisa and I are so incredibly busy with our family or business that we forget the small important things that have happened in our day. If we query each other, one of us is bound to say, "Oh, I forgot to tell you who I saw yesterday!" or "I forgot to tell you that your dentist appointment is tomorrow at noon." Interview your best friends as well as complete strangers. Make your business their second home.

The tour of the coffee roasterie creates amnesia, too. Five minutes of a quick coffee education brings comfort and peace to your soul and it may have been the easiest conversation that you've had all day long. Did I ask you, "What do you do for a living?" You told me and then I introduced you to other business owners in the cafe who could help you grow your business. Did you just move into town? Congratulations. Come over to the business card library and let me give you the contact information for people who can help you with your move or repairs. Regardless of whether we know what you do for a living or you're looking for work, we'll introduce regular customers to one another, just for fun. Hey Jane, have you met Sam? And that's Brad in the corner. Do you get introduced to strangers in any other coffee shop?

We build layer upon layer of community and comfort so that

1) we can improve your life financially and maybe even emotionally and

2) we want to empower you to help others with our connections and

3) happy and empowered customers create more customers for us and reduce our time and money in marketing and sales.

When we introduce you to our "favorite plumber," and he becomes your favorite plumber, you are going to share this favorite plumber with your friends and family. The plumber is now our best friend because we've put more money in his pocket and helped him grow his customer base. He can do what he does best and not spend time and money advertising his craft. The plumber purchases more coffee, tells his friends about our establishment and in effect, becomes our new salesperson. You, the customer, now feel great because the "favorite plumber" responded immediately to your plumbing issue, was reasonably priced, and did a great job. We added a layer of comfort to your life, saved you money, and we saved you time because you didn't have to hunt down a good plumber in the middle of the night. In addition, when you referred the plumber to your friend, the plumber and your friend appreciated the kindness that you did for them and they will be more thoughtful of ways to help you. The plumber may even give your friend a half pound of Chazzano Coffee because the plumber wants to share the love of his favorite coffee shop. The plumber, the customer, and the customer's friend are all now part of the sales force of Chazzano Coffee because of that first warm referral. How far can this scenario go? Usually too far for you to track. With one referral, with one introduction, you could possibly create 20 new salespeople for your company.

A company cannot survive without new customers every week. Customers die, move, change their diet, or become uninterested in your business for various reasons. If your regular customers don't rave like lunatics about your business, you're in trouble. I know people who rave about their favorite Italian restaurant. I am constantly accosted by customers I didn't know we had, who rave to me about Chazzano Coffee. Some friends rave about their favorite pediatrician. Others rave about their favorite wine shop. But who raves about their synagogue or church? Not one person I know has ever raved about their synagogue or church. Really, no one. Have you heard this one, "Mike, you need to come to my synagogue this Saturday. I love attending services there every week. The Rabbi gives awesome sermons- I feel like I learn something new every week; and the Cantor sings like an opera singer; really powerful voice. You feel like G-d is in the room. The congregation is crazy friendly. Too many people say hello to me every week, but it's better than the opposite happening." The fact that I've never heard anyone rave about their house of worship is partly the reason why I wanted to write this book. I want congregants to rave about their relationship with their clergy, with the new amazing friends they've made at the house of worship, and how great they feel when they attend services.

That's just one problem. The other very serious problem is that congregants don't bring visitors to their house of worship. They are not referring new business to their worship space.

Again, people die or move. How do you replace them with new congregants to support the community? Every day, our regular customers bring new customers to our cafe.

Their friends say, "My friend has been raving about your shop for years. I had to come and visit".

I say, "Do you have time for a tour? Thank you for coming in. Do you know that we deliver straight to your door?"

Every day, some social media site drew their attention to our business to force them to walk in. We have our customers' reviews (raves) on sites like Yelp, Google Places, and Facebook to bring new customers in. If you build it, they will come...but only when your regular customers share their love for your business and invite them to visit. Without a constant stream of new customers, businesses and organizations die.

The Third Lack: Follow Through

The third issue is follow-through. How do you change new visitors with objections into regular customers? You create a referral marketing approach to your selling. The tour, the educational tidbits, the interview process of asking them what they do for a living, the genuine smile, and the passion for what you are doing, will create solutions for their lives. Your business or synagogue will be part of the solution. At your synagogue, a member needs a babysitter. Immediately introduce someone in the congregation who may be able to babysit her children. You just built a network. The synagogue is now a place to help her grow her life and solve some of her problems. When a visitor comes to the synagogue, convince them to call after the Sabbath to reconnect.

Long time members of synagogues all have a story to tell about how the congregation came together for them for happy or sad occasions. For my son's Bar Mitzvah celebration, my wife and I decided to cook for all of the 200 people. It was a way to save money, keep our vegan kosher diet, and to be a dugma (an example) for the community. It was a huge job just shopping and purchasing the food. But making 22 trays of vegan lasagna, regular dairy lasagna, and other vegan dishes was even more time consuming. Scary stuff. However, one woman organized helpers to share the burden. We were able to finish all of the preparation in time for the Sabbath. The highest form of loving kindness was when the President of the synagogue and her husband, just the two of them, washed all of the dishes after the celebration and told us to just...enjoy.

Whatever happens in this synagogue community, we'll always remember the way our community assisted us. If a synagogue has hundreds of stories from members about how the synagogue has transformed their lives, that synagogue is healthy and growing.

The follow-through is found in the constant, loving education and interviewing of your clients, customers or congregants. Chazzano Coffee sells over 20 different coffees and over 75 different blends. Why? The reason is that we're addicted to awesome tasting coffee and we love learning about new coffees and new brewing methods. We already have loving regular customers, but we want customers who are constantly growing and learning. When we introduce a new coffee, and we ask them, "How does it taste?", we are giving them greater ownership of the business. When someone buys something from you, do you call them and say, how is everything? Were you happy with the service? Follow-through with congregants. Ask them, "So, you've been a member for three months, what do you most like about the synagogue, and what do you dislike the most? What's missing?" If you asked everyone those questions, you would lose very few members.

Do you know what I despise the most? It's worse than anti-semitism, racism, and baseless hatred. It's synagogue surveys. Instead of sitting down with people face to face, you hand them a survey about, "How are we doing?" Do you know who fills them out? For the most part it is the people who are unhappy. If the synagogue board sat down with their congregants, you would learn more about them as business people, individuals, and as fellow worshipers.

The Sages Say, A Smile Can Change the World

The secret of great customer service is smiling genuinely. When someone is upset with the service of your company, it is difficult for them to stay angry when you smile. If you're really smiling with genuine love, they will feel your sense of care. When I worked as an usher at the Metropolitan Opera House in Manhattan, I worked in the prestigious orchestra north section where some of the most expensive seats were found. Many movie and music stars would sit in my section of the theater. One of the greatest attributes of the Met was their cheap seats- you could stand for $10 a performance in the back of the orchestra section. One evening, a clearly mentally challenged woman in the standing room of orchestra

North began to scream before the performance and proceeded to attempt to pull out the hair of the woman seated in front of her. I grew up with a Jewish mother and an Italian Catholic father who loved me dearly but would scream at each other like lunatics frequently, so I knew how to remain calm under such circumstances. So, I walked over calmly with a smile and said, "Excuse me, could you please stop pulling the hair out of the woman in front of you? Would you please come with me?" The woman followed me and I handed her over to security. Sometimes, all it takes is a smile and a pleasant demeanor.

When someone walks into the cafe, our employees smile and quickly say "Hello, we'll be right with you" or "welcome, what can we get for you?" A smile gives people an acknowledgment that they are important to you. After I lead services during major Jewish holidays, the Rabbi and Cantor (me) wait for congregants to leave the sanctuary and we greet them with hearty smiles and wish them a happy holiday, tell them that we're grateful to see them, and we hope to see them soon. After smiling for about a half hour, my cheeks burn with overuse. How many times have your cheeks hurt from smiling for too long?

The Sages (the wise men of Jewish thought throughout the ages) have said, "One can change the world with a smile." When you walk down the street or pass a stranger in the supermarket and make eye contact accidentally or purposefully, do you smile? Why not? How awesome is it when your smile is returned with a bigger one? Sure, if there is a beautiful person, someone to whom you are attracted who smiles back, that definitely warms your soul. But, a child or someone who is much older than you returning a smile can also make your day. Some days it seems that your life is horrible. Everything seems to go wrong. Your employees are annoying you. Your cash flow is experiencing a severe drought. Yet, that young woman with a big frown on her face may be having the worst day of her life. She may have heard that her mom has cancer. Her boyfriend is cheating on her. All of her friends posted on Facebook that they're going out to eat, but no one invited her. Do you know how you can change her life? Smile through her frowns. Make a gentle joke. Give her a tour of your business or organization to take her mind off of her sorrow. Introduce her to other customers and tell her stories that you know about them. When you own a business, smiles will increase your revenue. People will want to come into the establishment when they're happy or sad. Regardless of their previous disposition, your establishment will be a place of comfort and belonging.

I'm a mischievous kind of guy. When I know that someone dislikes me, or my interpretation of their dislike is the product of their inability to look me in the eyes as if they have been telling everyone in the world how much they despise me, I do something very wicked. I smile. I seek them out and smile. I shake their hand, I act as if they are my favorite person in the world. I ask them how they're doing or feeling. I ask them if they are doing anything fun this weekend. How's work? How's the business? In short, I try to kill them with kindness. After this barrage of questions, I sometimes break their shell of dislike or apathy and they begin to treat me well. Sometimes, nothing changes and week after week after synagogue services, they continue to look away from me and shake my hand begrudgingly.

Rabbi Morton Geller, a brilliant Rabbi who was the spiritual leader of my in-laws' synagogue in Gloucester, Massachusetts, and the Rabbi who was the officiant at our wedding counseled the following. "Frank, remember this throughout your career. When they criticize you, don't take it personally. When they complement you, don't take it personally. It's not about you. It's about them." When someone comes into your synagogue with a frown or is seemingly unfriendly, it's never about you. It's about something happening in their lives. If you want to gain a life-long congregant, friend or customer, befriend them with a smile. Talk to them with harmless, unobtrusive small talk.

The beginning of customer service is that smile. Your happiness is infectious. Whenever I see someone unhappy as they walk into my cafe, I smile immediately and try to bring joy to their lives. When the unhappy customer walks out of my cafe with a smile, we have changed the world. We have grown our business and therefore we've grown our lives. In the Jewish synagogue service, Jews stand up three times each day to pray the "standing prayer." In our beginning conversation with G-d, we remind G-d about the connections that we've had-Abraham, Isaac, and Jacob, some Jewish patriarchs that were traditionally close to G-d. When I speak of this beginning blessing to Hebrew School students, I compare this to the first impression before we actually ask G-d for something. We "butter up" G-d saying that G-d is G-d on High, King, Helper, Savior, and Shield. In the same way, we may speak to our parents before we ask them for the keys to the car. For most people, that first impression, the first interaction, must begin with a smile.

I've learned a lot about business from my life as a synagogue Cantor, and as an observant Jew. In Jewish tradition, G-d gave us 613 commandments, rules by which to live. For those who believe in a G-d who gives specific commands to his people, they are commandments and not suggestions. Some of the first commandments are found in the story of Abraham and the three angels. First, although Abraham is convalescing under the shade of a tree after being circumcised at an advanced age, he stands up to greet three strangers who arrive at his tent and asks them to stay for a meal. This first commandment is to be a good host. When guests come to your home, you are commanded to be a good host. Make them comfortable, but also ask them about their well-being, and ask them how their family is doing. Have you ever been invited to someone's home and find that they are terrible conversationalists, and they really expect you to entertain them? They don't ask anything about you or why your spouse hasn't arrived yet. Although Abraham was ill, he recognized that the three men (angels) had been walking in the heat, and must require some food and water. The second commandment is taught when the angels ask Abraham's wife, Sarah, "How is your husband?" The guest has responsibilities, too. It is a commandment to ask about your host, your host's spouse, children, friends, or livelihood. I've always had crazy good interpersonal skills. But this passage from the Torah teaches us some framework for our interaction with others. It's a two way street of concern- the guest and the host are expected to ask, "How are you?" with conviction.

Spend your days with a smile on your face. See if you can change the world with a smile. I cannot begin to measure how many times I feel like I've given people hope with just a smile. That smile of yours will bring random acts of kindness. It will also change your world because smiling, happy people are successful people. Or at least that is what people believe about them. People want to be around successful people. Successful, happy people breed more successful and happy people. But most of all, they breed new customers and longtime customers who will purchase from you. That will lead to a better life for you and your family. And that will really make you smile.

Lessons of The Father

My father, of blessed memory, used to say, "Frankie, keep your eyes open, ears open, and mouth shut." My father was a bright man who was a functional illiterate. He learned to read a bit when my mother passed away because he needed to pay bills by writing checks. Writing, "Con Edison," on the check took a few achingly long minutes for him. He was probably an undiagnosed dyslexic before people understood the affliction. However, my father was also a natural born philosopher. There were many sayings, some appropriate and some inappropriate for some to hear, that emphasized his brilliant interpretation of the world.

"Frankie, keep your eyes open, ears open, and mouth shut." Listen to what other people say. Watch their body language. Have you ever seen a tall, gorgeous woman who slouches and just doesn't seem to have any self-confidence? I'm shocked often by that realization- they're drop dead gorgeous and their minds don't know it. Your eyes hurt because she's like a Greek goddess. On the other hand, have you seen someone who is a slob and unkempt who has tremendous confidence and poise? When you stop talking, and listen to others, and watch them carefully, you'll learn more about them. You may get to know what they love to do, their goals or their dreams. Be kind to everyone.

My father's kindness during one particular Thanksgiving provides a great lesson about the way you should treat everyone, working to grow your life and your business by making a community wherever you reside. It's one of my favorite memories of my father and it taught me about making people feel comfortable in their surroundings and making them feel like they are part of something greater than themselves alone.

My mother died in 1989 and my father remarried. My problem with spending Thanksgiving with my father is that he didn't live in a household that kept strict Jewish dietary laws (Kosher). My father loved me and wanted Lisa and me to spend Thanksgiving with him, his wife, and in-laws. He prepared a Kosher feast for us! Everything that one expects from a Thanksgiving meal was purchased from a Kosher butcher and he supplied plastic forks and paper plates. What makes this remarkable was not that he did this for his only son, his only child. He did this even though he felt that the Jewish side of my mother's family had slighted him throughout his life with my mother. To make someone feel included, you need to know what makes them comfortable. You may need to spend more money or more time, but they'll remember you forever.

The Fourth Lack: Integrity

The fourth issue that hurts the future of houses of worship is a lack of vision or integrity. If you accommodate everyone, you accommodate no one. If everyone is correct, no one is correct. At Chazzano Coffee, there is great flexibility in selections of coffee, brewing methods, and delivery methods. However, we are rigid in our mission. The title of this book, "G-d cries, and an angel loses its wings" is part of that rigidity. We want customers to live a healthier lifestyle without all of the added sugar and cream. We want to enrich their lives by having them change their default way of drinking coffee. Drink it black first. If it needs sugar, it's not your favorite cup of coffee; we'll give you another one to try. If it needs sugar, then you just don't like the flavor profile or it's stale.

Have you ever heard of a coffee shop that doesn't serve food? That's our shop. We want you to appreciate the different flavors that are found in fresh roasted coffee. If you had a piece of biscotti with that cup of coffee, you'd miss how awesome that cup of coffee would have been. Finally, how many coffee roasters give away unsold 2.5 week old coffee to homeless shelters because it's not fresh enough? Rigidity and integrity are integral to gaining respect for your organization. In every successful business, there are special standards for which they are known. Frank, will you ever serve food at Chazzano? Never.

Orthodoxy in any religion brings in new members because there is a certain level of respect and awe that is built in the fact that nothing really changes. They know what to expect every week. There is rigidity and integrity for a reason. Why do we do this particular ritual? Because G-d said so. That's enough information for many people. Orthodox means strict. It is the traditional way of doing. There is no room for reformation or any other names for it. It is strict. But Orthodoxy of every kind is often criticized for lacking love. It is okay to believe that your daughter should only marry your kind of Orthodox, but that doesn't mean that you're not allowed to smile at someone who has different beliefs from yours. This is the strict way that you have decided to live, but you can still help people who are in need of a smile, a helping hand, or some thoughtful advice. However, great respect is given to someone or to some organization that can pair love with integrity and rigidity of purpose.

This is what I do often. I am embarrassed to admit it, though. Often, after taking a few sips of the coffee that I roasted and brewed, I exclaim with a smile, "That is an awesome cup of coffee." I'm embarrassed because that should be the default expression that I have when tasting my own product. In fact, it is. I marvel at the quality and complexity of our coffee several times a day. For me, drinking coffee is not a caffeine fix- drinking 20 cups of coffee every day is the norm. Drinking coffee is a way to enrich my life by slowing it down. When I marvel that the Malawi Mindali Estate coffee has notes of blackberry, boysenberry, juniper berries, with a touch of cinnamon, I am taking the time to appreciate, to show gratitude for something special in my life. Do you love your business?

Now that I've shared one of my most embarrassing moments, here's why it's important to be living a life where you marvel at your own product or service daily. If you have that excitement, it will be transmitted to your clients or customers. When a preacher concludes her sermon and she says to herself, "That was a very good sermon. I'm proud of myself," that appreciation will be shared with her parishioners. When a chef tastes his barbeque sauce, and says, "It's impossible to find a better sauce," their customers will also love that barbeque sauce. The most important aspect of this self horn tooting is that you, the business owner, are satisfied. Who said, "You need to love yourself before you love someone else?" They're correct. In order to grow your life, you need to be self satisfied with your business. You need to have tremendous pride in the great things that you've accomplished. If you don't stop and say, "I just did a great job," you need to find where your passion truly lies.

One of the most famous sages of Jewish thought was quoted: "If I am not for myself, who will be for me? But if I am only for myself, who am I? If not now, when?" If you're thinking of ways to create a happy and healthy life for yourself and for your family, who else will care? No one, really. If you only think about how to grow your business and make more money, who are you? You won't be recognizable and people won't want to be with you. You won't connect with the right people who will help you grow your business and life. When you think only about yourself, people stop caring. And finally, if not now, then when? You need to start somewhere. Begin by smiling more. Then add a bit of education and storytelling. Then start interviewing complete strangers. Think about yourself first. Evaluate where you want to be next week, next month, next year or 10 years from now. Then, while remembering your goals, spend time fulfilling others' goals. Don't tarry, change your life now.

About the Author

Frank Lanzkron-Tamarazo was the Cantor of synagogues in New York, New Jersey, Illinois, and Michigan. He now serves as Cantor of Congregation Beth Shalom in Oak Park, Michigan. Frank is better known as the owner, founder, and Master Roaster of Chazzano Coffee Roasters in Ferndale, Michigan. Chazzano Coffee Roasters was founded in October 2006 and continues to win awards every year for Best Coffee Shop in Detroit, Best Tea Shop in Detroit, and Best of Ferndale. Frank has counseled numerous business owners, friends, employees, and the temporarily unemployed on how to grow their lives, and their businesses and most importantly, how to do what they passionately want to accomplish.

For more information, please visit God and Coffee Consulting's website:
www.GodandCoffeeConsulting.com

Made in the USA
Middletown, DE
11 January 2018